Winging It

Winging It

SYMPHONIC
POEMS

RIVKA EPSTEIN HATTIN

HEADSTAND
PRESS

movements.poems@gmail.com

ISBN 978-965-93207-3-8

Published by Headstand Press
Cover design by Natalie Friedemann-Weinberg & Rivka Epstein Hattin
Cover background photo by Meriç Dağlı on Unsplash
Author photo by Leeba Hattin
Book interior by Lindsay Lusby
Typeset in Adobe Caslon Pro, Adobe Hebrew, Vatican, and Bree

Printed in the United States of America

First Printing, 2025

Contents

DELECTABLES

FLESH

AMORE

CREATORS

LESSONS

BEYOND

EARTH

For Michael ~

The Song of My Songs

my dove that dwells
in the clefts of cliffs
in the hidden heights
let me find your face
let me savor your sound
for your voice is velvet
and your presence is pleasure

Shir HaShirim 2:14

desiring
eggs, divine eggs
to cure
my frigid blues

awaiting
that flitting
balance beam barista
her brilliant beans
her Jaffa fruit

satiating
this sandwich mama
the belly's thanksgiving song
bursts forth, gracing Earth

gratitude is a dew
a wet kiss
toward Heaven

Delectables

Divine Eggs

make me an omelet
moons of purple onion
splattered with wild mushrooms
a sprig or two of parsley
crumbled feta

not burned like my ego
not raw like my nerves
but simmering with the possibility of satiety

Frigid Blues

when love lies rancid
on the bottom shelf
her hand is drawn
to toss it
clear space
believing the delivery man
will indeed arrive

when love lies rancid
on the bottom shelf and the guests
arrive early
banging the brass knocker

when love lies rancid on the bottom shelf
and the fridge has nothing to serve

Balance Beam Barista

dare not wobble
balance beam barista
serve up danger
teeter
tea with cream please
don't fall too
far
down your coffee's
ready
steady your arms
above your head
orbiting black clouds
with blazing reach
teach us how to
balance beam barista

special today
Guatemala roast
side of toast
dip down
toes point of view
nothing will be fresh
footing, don't lose your footing
dare to wobble
table topple
bill now please
balance beam barista

Jaffa Fruit

The first time I tasted a fresh fig
I was sweating like a pig
on holy ground.

The thick aroma of an almost petite aubergine,
innocent fun,
splitting her open with a tender tug—
pink bobbly innards, tight and smug.

I slurped that nectar,
divine elixir.
The life juice of prophets and poets,
rulers and misfits,
crusaders, invaders,
drooling pontificators.

Woe unto thee
in that moment of immaculate consumption—
the heavens shifted,
copper and violet hues,
firmaments drifted.

And the clouds assembled
rumbling, troubling—
first dropping, then drenching—
unforgiving, yet cleansing.

I was afloat but just barely,
clutching the side of that wobbly craft—
so needy,
still greedy.

The last time I gobbled a fig,
a giant fish swallowed me whole,
the night stars fell beneath me—
curled upside down, broken and low.

On the grainy golden shore,
purple skins poking south
of my puckered mouth—
new verses, fresh lore.

With a beached whale beside
us two fruits, Jaffa's pride
to be picked by the gulls—
once life, now skulls.

Sandwich Mama

I am the bread of freedom.
I am woman.
I am the bread of affliction.
I am mother.
I am leavened. Unleavened.
Kosher. Cracked.
Often nourishing, sometimes brittle.
Often whole, sometimes burnt.
THE SAND WITCH
Heschel called man dust and image.
THE SANDWICH
Hillel called it the temple.
I am daughter.
I am child.
A BLESSING
Before.
A BLESSING
After.
On the whole.
What a blessing.

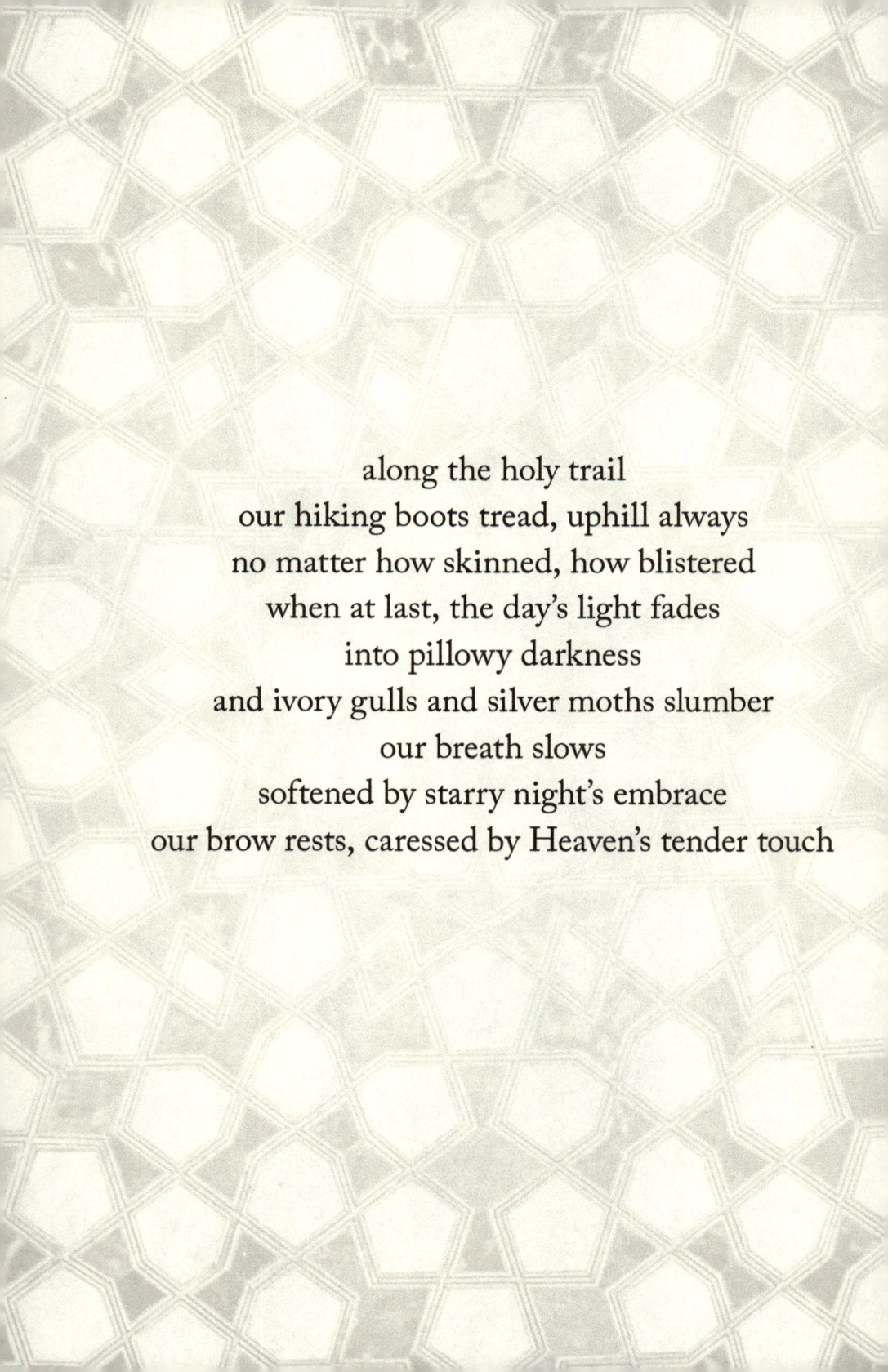

along the holy trail
our hiking boots tread, uphill always
no matter how skinned, how blistered
when at last, the day's light fades
into pillowy darkness
and ivory gulls and silver moths slumber
our breath slows
softened by starry night's embrace
our brow rests, caressed by Heaven's tender touch

Flesh

Holy Trail

When the muscles balk
after the kettlebell falls heavy
from a long round
gritsweatpantcursegrowl
with sullen eyes and agitated voice, exclaim—
"You push me beyond. I quake. You are unrelenting."
I pause.
I have indeed demanded of this sinew, this tissue,
to rip herself,
tear deep on my behalf.
My herculean crusades march forth
with little regard for the tattered sheathing
under the winter blankets of flesh.
These are the tiny deaths
scattered along the holy trail,
mile markers oblivious to others.
I pause, aware
that muscle is as limited and limitless
as mind.

Hiking Boots

My hiking boots
give me back
twenty-five years.
I lace them up—the loopydoopy smile of
red strings.
I bounce off wet, mossed
boulders like a boss,
leap above the rushing
white frothy waters—
no fear,
no mortgage,
no tomorrow.

Right now,
there are light spears piercing the forest pines.
Right now,
the sheer granite mountaintops vault above green velvet valleys.
Right now,
my ears burst with nature's *sturm und drang* cacophony.

My worries are cleansed—
a spanking wet baby, out of the tub—
fresh glee, gushing hope.
My hiking boots
are coming with me to the grave.

Skinned

I am a fierce arrow, shot wild without target,
skateboarding barefoot, rushing along the shoulder,
dry throat, wet armpits pitted against howling wind,
the tumbling wheels churning speed under trembling toes.

I am a fierce arrow, shot wild without target,
can't sound my alarm, crack this jaw, even tongue thrust.
Tears burn these cheeks, leaded silence weighs these thighs.
Justice, I beg. I've done right. The road scoffs, narrows.

A cloud drops ahead, prayer returned to sender.
How heavens dump unwanted trash, little remorse.
How feet feel the fire beneath, yet take no heed.

Ode to the Wizard

to Lior

The sheep-shearing wizard—
his cave door opens to the bustling boulevard,
but inside the dark cavernous hole,
only mirrors refract light,
warming the space that assures those entering
that they shall emerge within the hour more alive than before.
Their gray strands of mortality, beneath his elixirs, will vanish,
replaced with the promise of eternity—
for a pittance of a fee, really—
and all the while, his mouth is running:
balms for the brokenhearted,
salves for the unsalvageable,
the victims of life's cruel vicissitudes.
Such a small fee, really,
that pays for itself considering the longevity he sells—
even as the tresses are trimmed,
the hairdresser vanquishes the ticktock clock,
lock by lock,
as days past are returned, reversed,
as time inverts.
Same time next month, baby doll?

Farewell, Mother Teresa

Farewell, Mother Teresa.
Your swollen feet need a pedicure.
Your extended hand needs a mitten.
Your growling belly needs a steak.

Farewell, Mother Teresa.
Your bank account needs attention.
Your English garden needs bulbs.
Your bay window needs a schpritz.

Farewell, Mother Teresa.
The cruise ship has docked.
The dancing girls have boarded.

Pick up your ticket.
Time to boogie on the seas.

Silver Moth Slumber

blankets of purple sky
kiss her lined brow
hoist her through
narrow tunnels
of slumber
enter a world of other
oiled portraits and orchid gardens
born for a snippet
like the silver moth that zooms
across a room just once
leaving but the memory
of flight

blankets of broken black
brush her soft face
send her off to dungeons
she dares not revisit
next gilded palaces

dreams
a night treasure box
packed for her alone
the rare rainbow that floats
above the heavy soil
leaving but the memory
of light

Cast

My mind is an ear
choosing flute song at dawn.
My mind is an eye
plucking gold coins from the dandelion sun.
My mind is a broken foot
that can't be cast.

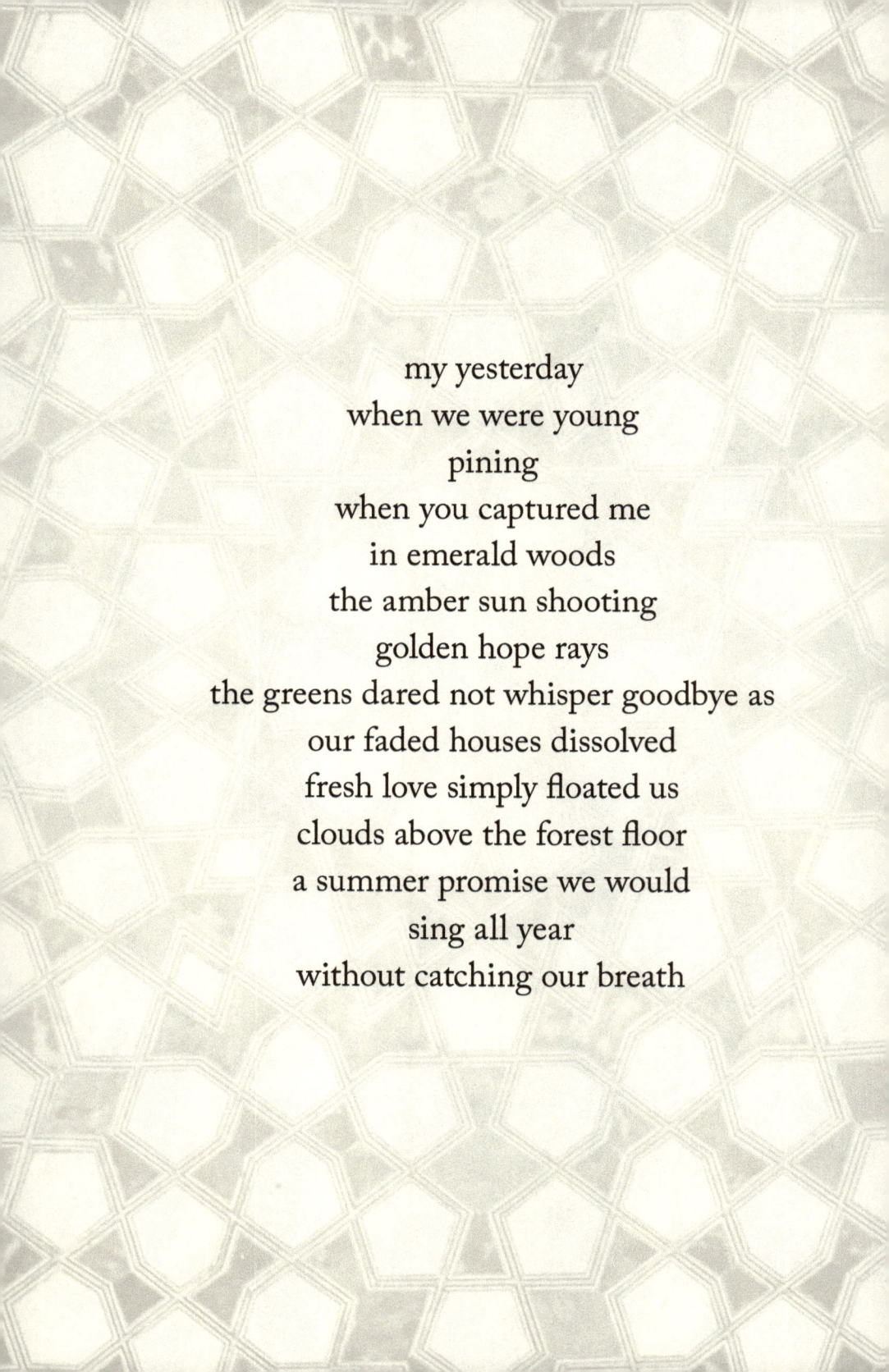

my yesterday
when we were young
pining
when you captured me
in emerald woods
the amber sun shooting
golden hope rays
the greens dared not whisper goodbye as
our faded houses dissolved
fresh love simply floated us
clouds above the forest floor
a summer promise we would
sing all year
without catching our breath

Amore

My Yesterday

hairball,
your scratchy chin prickles
my velvet cheek but
kiss me deeply

pungent thing, your sweaty grip slips
round my arched back but
embrace me tighter

cataract eyes, your searching gaze almost lands upon
my wanting face
find me, devour me

you are my yesterday
and we will
tomorrow

Young in Pine

beneath the friendly shadow
of this towering pine
you take your muscled arm and wrap it around mine

planted perfect in this meadow
as my humming watch nears nine
you bring your moist lips close and halt my breath and time

Capture Me

My iridescent radiance
through the lens,
your kindest lens.

Hold me, the whole of me,
as large, as impossible, to grasp.

Fly me, over memories
spanning worlds,
even if the seas below us
stretch on, stretch on,
beneath our solid wings.

Travelers say farewell
once they have discovered the glory
and tucked it safely away.
Safely away.

Whisper Goodbye in My Ear

Whisper goodbye in my ear.
      No, no—don't.
Face me and say it clear.
Let the final words stand upright.
Allow me to reach my hesitant hand out
and clutch them—tight to each corner of sound
pressed to my breast.

I can grip that goodbye
while walking through town squares we should be strolling
together
but will not share again.

Whisper goodbye.
      No, no—sing it,
as your eyes lock mine
and your chocolate voice keeps me company
in memories of melodies that welcomed harmonies
graciously
as a warm empty nest that just waits,
waits to be full.

Our song soars
like a fire-winged eagle,
never touching down.
Whisper goodbye, yes, whisper
to love that must—but cannot bear—to end.

Amber Sun

When he noticed her, the ivory moon froze
as the late-night hour stretched her back,
lullabies purred open hearts a crack.
When longing moves stone, it grows and it grows
beyond daffodils' reach, past rhyme, past prose,
beyond ruby-red jewels in a thick velvet sack.
This is love, he swore, you will never lack.

When he noticed her, the amber sun rose—
but Longing—she trots, not steady nor sure.
Dark stallions, untamed, know best the night's force.
Passion bleeds wild as the blackest horse,
trampling soft young hearts, no matter how pure.
There were quick glances for years, but of course
her scent, amber sun, still stings with allure.

The Way

the way I love
is with three hands
one cups your cool chin
one presses your velvet palm
one drops generous coins into your back pocket while you
    laugh, eyes shut

the way I forgive
is with three breaths
one blows away the bitter chaff from the righteous stalk of
    indignation
one cools the ruby-red flames of rage
one resuscitates hope after she's fallen flat on the bedroom
    tiles

the way I believe
is with three souls
one digs up rusty miracles from the overgrown garden
one waits patiently for sunrises that may arrive after noon
one tangoes, wet with sweat, on the front porch for no
    reason at all

Summer Me

luscious mangoes
drip
brush my shoulder
out falls an opportunity missed
crystal sprinkles
a ride
that flips, turns, twists upside down
faster than a shriek exploding
hot-pink halter
sun-kissed skin

summer me
smother me
in cotton candy at the fair
throw me high but don't
catch me on the low
drown me in glitter
gifted from above
the late-hour fireworks bathe
me in lemonade
eternal apricot sunsets
don't touch down

summer me
in blazing sand
lime-green sea
crunchy shells
catching between the toes
and the treasure a
scribbled note
professing
hot-pink
first
love

the masters of color
magicians
word-weavers
song-spinners
mothers of clay
birthing wet lumps of hope
that take shape
take flight
take breath away
they nurse dangling vines of hope
that stretch
that grab
meaning is born
like a flaming drum
spreading haunting tones and images
branding our memories
creations, these wildfires,
burn for eternity

Creators

Flaming Drum

Memory is a flaming drum,
tossing her streaks
on beat
at one, at two, at three.

Memory is a burning gourd,
shaking her fire to free
herself, blistering others
at one, at two, at three.

Grab the sheets!
The wet towels!
The half-full jug!

One! Two! Three!
Douse earth. Douse door.
Drench and pour!
Redeem me. Redeem memory.
At one, at two, at three.

Piano Wars

When
the dark, the light,
ebony, ivory,
jail
the hammering sounds,
crashing wood
splinters silence,
unleashing torrential tidal waves—
metal coils gyrate
like drunken truckers
spinning on black ice,
pitches trapped in the oaken dungeon—
who rules this empire of cacophony?
who wins?

Nuance

That there's no word in Hebrew for NUANCE—
it's not an accident.
Israelis pride themselves on the
> *DUGREE—*
a word that means
tell it like it is.
Supposedly, at EYE LEVEL
(but it hits below the belt).
If it stings, it means it's healing you.
The truth sets you free, hon.
YOU ARE WAY TOO SKINNY.
YOU ARE INCOMPETENT.
YOU are taking the parking spot I eyed from three blocks away and deserve since my father fought in three Israeli wars and you can't pronounce one guttural consonant without sounding like you're choking on a
CHICKPEA.
Who the hell asked you to move here anyhow?

The word NUANCE:
a light string quartet of sound
like clinking porcelain teacups on a Sunday morning
or the rise in slightly arched eyebrows.
Like the rare summer rain shower catching you unawares
or the op-ed that is tickling you with its benign complexity.
Like the delicate scent of eucalyptus in a polished antique shop
and the manicured grass of sprawling green gardens, open for
    all.
I wonder:
Can nuance survive in the desert?

For Clay

Slippery wet clay,
I pray
you'll permit me
to mold, stretch, dry you
into a sturdy vessel.
Not lopsided,
not ordinary,
but glistening in your glory glaze,
inviting passersby to reach out,
hold you,
caress you,
treasure your smoothness,
your straightness,
your eternity.
      Yes,
      it's eternity I ask for.

Hope Is a Dangling Vine

When hope is a dangling vine
and I, the explorer, hunt for morning glory,
I feel doubt of her many promises.
I sit tinkering in my cave
where music is birthed and breath restored.
I come into the comfort of sound.
I come into the shores of first creation,
warmed by hot breezes that reach earth from sky,
begging me to stay longer. I rest in melodies unheard,
      then sing.

Hapax Legomenon

the endangered species
of words
caged in solitude
to be viewed once
at great expense
don't sneeze or snooze
or you'll miss its fleeting
exhibitionism

In a Lullaby

if I kept my life
in a cloud
it might blow away to Nicaragua

if I kept my life
in a basket
it might sail down the Nile

if I kept my life
in a lullaby
it might sing itself into oblivion

if I kept my life
in a classroom
it might outsmart itself

if I kept my life
in a vacuum
it might swell beyond measure

Unordinary Art

How funky art thou,
you standard goldfish!
One half hour with Picasso
and you will be cubically immortalized.

How graceful art thou,
fuzzy market peach.
One hour with Cézanne and your golden skin will glow.

Waterlilies will sing arias.
Biceps will vanquish demons.
Monet and Rodin
will not let us down.
Oh no.

Brushing fantastical possibilities into tomorrow,

I ask you this:
Is the artist's work as essential to
our sinking souls
as a life jacket tied to
a bloated goldfish?

Plumbing

writing is the plumbing
running the watery brain through the throbbing heart
channeling through narrowing pipes
as it bursts
busy fingers sprinkle words
furious faucets
shooting out meaning, washing away assumption
irrigating minds
refreshed, even purified

Meaning Is Born

When meaning crowns
like two palms,
it is shared,
warming two bodies
on a frosty night.

A cavity must open,
air flows,
muscles contract—
sound is born
but not meaning.

Reception is conception
when words embrace.
Because they are heard.
Because they are spoken.
Because they are hallowed,
refused, ridiculed,
cataloged, corked, misconstrued,
stretched, skipped, studied,
turned to song, turned to feed, turned to dust.

When words
falter,
then stand upright, spread, proliferate
with the guilty pleasure
of independence,
protest,
seduction,
clarity.
When words walk out the door
as pencil scribbles in a desert tent
and find themselves waltzing atop a kitchen table across the
bay.

They change that day
hardened molasses finally runs free.
When ears, eyes, mouth, mind
devour and delight
in the sport.
Why, it's in that
union,
liberation,
that
meaning is born.

Words in Waiting

Before I open my crusted eyes,
the words wait,
nip
my lips,
drag my smile up the wooden steps.
Those words read:
"Good morning, raiser of the flag!"
My trusted friend
texts me
earlier than lit sky,
earlier than sparrows find their wings,
earlier than lanes teem with fuming company.
You see, it's curious
because
I actually only raised the flag once.
But she remembers it. Frames it.
Perhaps because it means that gravity
is not the end of the story and, before I open my crusted eyes,
the words wait.

Well, You Invited Her!

ode to the poetry muse

like your Aunt Bertha
she shows up unannounced
makes a fuss about all that sun in the guest room
tosses a few flowery gifts around
likes her espresso straight up
and with that soaring heart rate
takes you for a rodeo that leaves you wailing
like a babe at midnight hour

who believes
in test-tube
boys
in hope
in Harlem
the unmapped hunt
is a teacher
like grief
its largeness
can swallow us whole

Lessons

Test-Tube Boy

Test-tube boy, he was called.
Biology texts his bedtime stories—
embryos and embolisms,
not tribalism nor hedonism.
His pencil parents, wringing hands, fretting over his potential
energy lost in the velocity of maturation—
if their genius son fell
in a wood with no one to hear,
would he still make honor roll?
The test-tube boy, he was called, even as they laid
him in Harvard Yard, second year.
The vibrant mind with no motion—a boy at rest
tends to stay at rest.

Newborn

when prayers hang from the sky
reach beyond yesterday, pluck fruits of choice
the genius of the newborn is not asking why

though memory can choke the air supply
stifling dance and silencing voice
when prayers hang from the sky

the deep diggers, muddied boots, soaked in lye
live unafraid of crossroads and rattling noise
the genius of the newborn is not asking why

the mining men force their gazes high
when serpents lurk behind frolicking boys
when prayers hang from the sky

questions drop like laundry to dry
tempting the feeble, like lollies and toys
the genius of the newborn is not asking why

pack up those damning doubts, with dignified poise
toss them to sea, to sink, to lie
when prayers hang from the sky
the genius of the newborn is not asking why

Especially Now

You
Source
ברוך
Knocking on the golden oak door
of the red-bricked mansion
promising entry to the court
of heavenly rapture
on 48th St.

Mystery to me
אתה יקוק
We're tourists, he almost whispers,
his deeply lined brow descending further over his flaming beard.
The glass of lemon water between us.
The holy writ splayed atop a creamy silk cloth.

Ruler of my days
אלקינו
His smile rises.
    The dirtied boulevards are of no matter—we leave at dawn.
His inking words slap the leathered parchment
indelible.

Dominating my doubts

מלך

Masters know the art
of weeding untruths while the village sleeps,
leaving pastures manicured with a wink.

Shown and hidden

העולם

Above gray, salty-teared seas, beyond scented fields of myrtle.

Dripping dew

שהחיינו

Granting sun

וקיימנו

Harvesting together

והגיענו

In every season

לזמן

Especially

הזה

Now

Toasted

to large noses
flat feet
ADHD
imagination freed

to genes
we wrung hands over
that bore trophies
at kilometer 21

to colorblind eyes
chromosomes' disguise
the genius of the species
prize or demise

to not knowing
but glowing
to fear
when it's left to simmer

to yesterday's doubts
disperse!
hot tub hope
immerse!

to truth
flapping her crimson skirt
stomping her strut
shouting 'til hoarse
I'm here, in red!

to applause
when it roars louder than our errors
to the rise, the drop
the heft, the flop

to not knowing, but glowing
to fear when it's left to simmer

to swallowing seawater
when flailing, still swimming
dimming colorblind eyes
chromosomes' disguise

to knowing, but slowing
but slowing
still glowing
glowing

Largeness

There are those who tower.
Their great shadows
fall,
blocking light,
blocking.

There are those who take up space.
Two parking spots for
one compact car,
hogging spots,
hogging.

There are those whose voices dominate,
cancel rebuttals before utterance,
squelching speech,
squelching.

Then, there are those who vacate,
who allow,
who invite.

Creating light,
opening space, igniting discourse.

There are those:
LARGER, yet shadowless.

Hope in Harlem

The trip starts late
on a train to the south Bronx,
last stop.

I don't make it.
We are all alone in the car.
His eyes ogle me from the start.
As he inches closer,
his yellow crooked smile
toys with my heart rate,
reaching his bony fingers towards my suitcase handle,
gripped, white-knuckled, like I am holding my whole life
in a locked sweaty palm.

His cracking voice insists
on carrying my bag.
Those huge eyes—sweeping over my body,
moving too close, feeding off my fear.
The sickly sweet smell of urine fills my nostrils.

Whose?

There's one more stop.
Run, my mothervoice insists.
He'll follow me, whines my inside child.
Dart out the door now, into the Harlem night.
Who is waiting out there?

I hurl myself down the iron stairway, a sorrowful beast in a
    sudden stampede.
His hot breath licking my neck.

Damn, why can't I pack light?

She appears out of nowhere.
The tattoo lady. Head to toe.
No skin on her that's unrecorded,
cave walls that celebrate survival.
Will you help me? I plead.
I don't know whose voice I use.
It's helpless and an octave higher and I don't come in that flavor.
She meets my eyes.
I will stay with you until you are safe.
She must rehearse being the messiah daily.

A Teacher Called Grief

in silence
creeping on toe
invading

the tentacles
squeezing breath
stealing peace

a night thief
stashing sun
no remorse

an iron shackle
strangling ankles into
stone stillness

oh please, rush her
crazed swordsman
topple her mercilessly

eyes plead louder than cries
as salvation dissipates
like dew in the desert

this war drags
its heavy legs
a march toward eternity

this rickety bridge
delivers unknown selves
to foreign soil

grief
first reaper
then teacher

welcome
to Café Himalaya
raise your shot glass
to madmen, monsoons, mountains
manic markets
welcome
stuffed-duffle youth
seekers and saviors
trek onward to the fabled
other side

Beyond

Café Himalaya

Monsoons for supper,
peppered with a splash.
Monsoons for breakfast,
bubbling and brash.
A side of lightning.
Pickled. Frightening.
Crackles hissing.
Stirring. Fizzing.
Monsoons for tea.
Cardamom. Honey.
Do you like yours
served at midnight
or dawn?

Himalayan salt,
raw or browned?
Hold the fog?
Crushed chocolate log?
Americano? Macchiato?
Creamed or steamed
with coconut milk,
liquid silk?

Monsoon for fun,
a landslide or two,
a village awash—
first sailor, then crew.
Monsoon turned sour,
a flood, a sea.
Monsoon,
be kind
to them,
to me.

Raising

When your daughter
takes you to India
and,
lacing her fingers
into yours,
locks her heart into place,

skips toward the Taj Mahal,
her giggles bouncing in step,
raising you
as you raised her.

When your daughter
takes you to India
and feeds you yellow soup
and you pour her cardamom tea
and she floats on still waters
like a sea maiden whose strong arms reach
you as you reach her.

When your daughter takes you,
be taken.

Duffle

My worn canvas bag
is overstuffed
with Zen.

I bought it in bulk
in Dharamkot—
wrinkled rupees,
paper-thin greens
traded in the dark
dank kiosk
named Himalayan Oath.

The lanky hollowed seller,
his onyx eyes mellow,
muttering low, counting slow.

I bought Zen aplenty,
a fortune. Ten. No—twenty.
Because it's not fresh in my
neck of the woods.
So, yes, I splurged.
OK, I ODed.
On Zen. I did.

I pray to Shiva
and Lord Bagsu—
have mercy
at customs. Don't
confiscate Confucius
or I'm screwed.

Dharamkot Market

polished planets
orchid purple gems
flaunting themselves
ornaments, delighting
in these last summer rays
before the shadows win

stalls held together
by the sheer force of the
precarious
bamboo poles and
shady burlap

protecting sellers and luring buyers
paying for the half-innocent sport
in breathless frenzy

the scent of rosewater and ginger tea
the choking smoke
of incense
curling

the itch of llama wool shawls
and the caress of cashmere wraps

the glare of shined brass bowls
the blare of meditation pots
calling souls to humbly crouch

the grinning mirages
working their spells on
captive crowds
weighed down by coins
soon enough surrendered
for hand-stitched blood-red carpets
peace treaties
changing hands
for a moment

out on a limb
suspended and waiting for
winter's kiss
choosing this air
suspended and waiting for
sea swell
gray pigeon's crossing
sunflower's leave
suspended and waiting for
fuchsia's stirrings
virgin calls
September's fugue
convincing shells to open themselves
so life can crawl out
fearless or foolish
pausing for thunder but marching forth still
convinced that Earth will spin
again

Earth

Out on a Limb

I went out on a limb to rediscover my son.
I found fruit on the end of that limb—
a ripe possibility that promised sweet.

Roots in the jungle are wobbly.
Little did I know
how their rubbery, dancing shoots declare
flexibility will save them.
I thought that strength was hard, stiff stuff.
But in the jungle, it's the water—the liquid that is everywhere
as mist,
as sudden rainshower,
as rushing streams,
as filler of greens—
that is the promise of tomorrow.

Indiana Thunder

when shadows tangle
and dappled darkness traces light
feigning first innocence
a black pen
in unforgiving stroke
inks the sun

too suddenly
the horizon greens
unwanted pea soup

Indiana thunder

cracks my heart open
fear burns
through my nostrils
like silver lightning

When We Listen to September

the taunting call
of the mocking myna bird
at sunset red
the aching whine
of the pure white birch at windy dusk
the angry rumble
of empty-bellied soldiers returning
from too-long night duty
the first smack
of drip-drop autumn rain
upon a perfectly clear windshield

'Tis the Season

Elul is a two-faced time.
Some days
are sublime,
exploring edges
of the divine.
But
there are moments
reeking of guilt,
rains of regret,
black veils of shame
declaiming the same
Words, Words, Words
that pelt
the conscience.
Pages, Pages, Pages
that flip
through memory,
  that flaming pomegranate—
through fear,
  ramming its horns—
through loss,
  crying fish-eyed tears.

Above, Above, Above
reigns hope,
a honeyed elixir.
Elul is a two-faced
time.

Sunday's Fugue

The mare swayed
in the sawdusted corner,
tossing the shavings
toward the leaded heavens,
catching the August blanket of heat to cover her newborn
    foal, heaped
in the center of the stall,
his rapid beat pulsing through his heaving
belly, the air bubbling through
his thin, white, velvet skin as though
breath were a question, hesitantly asked.

My daughter Mir got the frantic
call at daybreak:

The barn is unlocked.
Refusing to nurse.
Legs too weak.
We may lose him.

I trotted behind her,
mother trailing teen,
her steeled gaze
far ahead of me,
determined to raise
the near-dead.
My shock
iced my mouth shut
as she darted through the stable,
knowing.

Mama Chocolate—

Kissing and kissing again her high neck,
murmuring in her dancing ear:

You warrior, you
birthed perfection.
Sweet Summer Dawn,
we'll call him
Sunday's Miracle.
Or do you prefer
Judean Prince?

They nuzzled noses as
the foal found his feet.
Mir caught the white belly beneath, guiding
the wobbly newborn's
quivering lips, leaning up toward
his mama's
heavy, honeyed milk.

I knew to blend back into
the wooden walls.

Parents can hold up
the roof, if they say less.

The splat of dripping breasts
weeping, the floor awash
in worry-soaked hay.

The sun hung itself out to dry
like muddied work boots.
At last,
the quick rhythm she thirsted for,
the snowy colt's gulps
brought a slow grin upon her face
as my girl looked toward me.

In that bronzed moment,
our Sunday quartet
sounded an exalted encore known
to mothers and new life alone—
a fugue found
in nature's most private
corner.

A Sunflower's Leave

what's left
is drooping dry
her crusty leaves
collapsing
down down
that convincing smile
that electric yellow hello
returned to her maker
how she delighted us
when she stood upright
proclaiming that vitality
can triumph gravity
aflame then extinguished
a lady knows when to exit

Choose Air

sleeves of feather
flutter into the day
take flight, lifting off and up
it is possible to ascend
to peer at teeming lanes with calm
curiosity because you are floating above
with that freedom smile
that drives you

flutter into the day
with an open beak, cracked wide to receive
the feed others offer
graciously swallow, thankful
knowing adventures are born when mouths unlock
willing, daring

flutter into the day
as a creative
creature with color
winged
light

a bird in motion
that can land, indeed
but chooses air

Gray Pigeon

Wretched bird,
wing hanging like a loose tooth,
dangling—
rush, hobble, hobble, rush.

Scurrying across the porch—
rush, hobble, hobble, rush.
Trapped between four sheer walls,
windows that flaunt freedom
and mock flight.

The pace quickens
as the dead ends abound.
No exit. No chance.
The gray pigeon stuck low
as the azure heavens rise high,
as the sun ascends in an arc that smiles upside down
in false promise.

Rush, hobble, hobble, rush.
A flightless bird is prey—
pigeon gray, pigeon gray,
rush hobble, hobble rush.

A broken bird is a dead dog—
rush, hobble, hobble, rush, gray end.

When Fuchsia Stirs

that time of day
when fuchsia stirs
stretches herself
the rose goddess
dripping color
like melted wax
along the roadside
aflame
with summer scent
the noon hour strikes
her copper bell
and the amber queen bee
intoxicated, crazed dancer
hurtles forward toward the petals
beckoning
it's all honey now
topaz dew
flowing forth
it's all liquid love

Weather or Not

talk to tornadoes
they are twisted
but they do touch
down on towns
and spin a good tale

hang out with hurricanes
they do hit
but Hugo, Hilda, and Hazel
are tropical babes

soothe a tsunami
they are swell
but they wave
at the worst times

Shelly: Her Story

she lay there
whole
therefore proud
the journey through
tempest
torrents
tides
could not sand her
down
could not chip her
sound resolve

she lay there
sprawled
a casual treasure
collected upon whim
fancied
fingered for a flash
tossed easily
down

she lay there
to be sure
to be chosen
to be returned

Virgin Call

the very first call
a wet-feathered fledgling
gaping-mouthed
cries
perfectly pierces the canopy
trumpeting new life
nothing that has been sung before or after will match this
audacity
virgin bird song
paper-thin fluttering
with fresh passion
the delicate goddess
has never witnessed her own sound
the freedom of not knowing the whole of her glory
is the genius of the newborn

Sea Swell

sea swell
birthed unnoticed
deep beneath the turquoise
marbling surface
undulating unabashed
only at cusp, at seam
between salted flow and swallowing sands
far too late
there is only to leap over, past the crest
there is only surrender
and why not
laugh into the wind
the sound as lead will sink
the secret of births unnoticed
unleashing furies down the line
unstoppable

Spin Again

When sea-green soup meets crusty bay,
when lapping tides kiss earth away,
when snow-white gulls skim frothy waves,
then the day is full.

When toasty winds breathe down the back,
when starlit skies shine velvet-black,
when silver owls call dawn to crack,
then the night is drawn.

When all that crawls and all that wails,
when all that sings and all that sails,
when Earth does share its thousand tales,
then the world does spin
again.

Afterword

We are only as real as the throbbing heart.
I invite you to raise your palm, resting it upon that beat,
the pulse,
the inner metronome—
uniquely ordered, singularly rhythmic—
that only you feel.

That pulse is a promise.
Not the guarantee of wealth or longevity or even serenity,
rather it is the promise that
you are here, as sure as the red juice flows,
fully feeling your existence—
and, oh, you are a blessing.

Blessings are generative:
They grow the self. They grow others.

Mind the heart.

To you, who supported me, writing this diary of the heart:

Living, fighting, and losing loved ones throughout this hellish war has been transformative, and I am grateful to those who have been beside me: sometimes forcing our fingers to play, sometimes lifting the load, sometimes singing along, sometimes crying together, sometimes feeding the troops, sometimes boogying in the holiday kitchen, sometimes lighting memorial candles on fresh graves, sometimes throwing wild parties, sometimes convincing each other to believe, sometimes begging until hoarse in prayer, sometimes scaling snowy mountains, sometimes giving our last dimes to keep each other alive, sometimes nursing our broken bodies into movement again, sometimes sharing our poetry.

I give you my precious love and infinite thanks.

Rivka

Alon Shvut

April 23, 2025

About the Author

Rivka Epstein Hattin is the author of two poetry collections, *Movements* and *Winging It*. She has also composed two hit musicals, *Talking to the Wall* and *Esther and the Secrets in the King's Court*. A beloved music teacher, Rivka explores sound and rhythm with budding artists of all ages. Together with Michael Hattin, their five kids, and two grandkids, she lives in a bopping treehouse, where music and words are the steady diet. Before a full day of pianists wafting through the door, Rivka delights in long runs through the terraced hills, fierce coffees, and headstands on the roof.